D1646444

THE
MOST AMAZING

CAT
VIDEOS EVER!

First published in Great Britain in 2015 by Prion Books

an imprint of the
Carlton Publishing Group
20 Mortimer Street
London W1T 3JW

Copyright © 2015 Carlton Books Limited

This book is sold subject to the condition that it
shall not, by way of trade or otherwise, be lent,
resold, hired out or otherwise circulated without
the publisher's prior written consent in any form
of cover or binding other than that in which it is
published and without a similar condition,
including this condition, being imposed upon
the subsequent purchaser. All rights reserved.

A CIP catalogue for this book is available
from the British Library.

ISBN 978-1-85375-941-3

Printed and bound by CPI Group (UK) Ltd, Croydon CR0 4TY

10 9 8 7 6 5 4 3 2 1

THE
MOST AMAZING
YouTube
CAT
VIDEOS EVER!

THE COOLEST, CRAZIEST AND
FUNNIEST INTERNET KITTY CLIPS

PRION

"I would never guess people would watch
cats do stupid things all day long."

George Lucas

INTRODUCTION

Far and away the world's Number 1 video-sharing platform, YouTube celebrated its tenth birthday in February 2015. Every month, over six billion hours of video are watched around the globe.

Not all of these are cat videos, but they do make up a significant proportion, as more and more people discover what can now truly be described as a thriving industry in its own right. Today there several bona fide superstar cats – the Cat Pack – and there are even dedicated festivals and award ceremonies to recognize the most accomplished examples of feline footage.

This collection charts the unstoppable rise of cats on the internet. Inside you'll find a selection of global viral hits, some of the most adorable and crazy cats on YouTube today, as well as a host of inventive and lesser-known spins on this fast-moving genre.

Whether you are a confirmed cat video addict, a budding "social petworker" checking out the competition, or simply curious about why people find watching cats on the internet so hard to resist, you'll find clips in this selection to entertain and delight.

Cute, cool, heroic, mind-boggling – and always unpredictable – this is a celebration of a phenomenon that is very much of the twenty-first century: the YouTube cat video.

INAPPROPRIATE LANGUAGE WARNING

The videos selected in this book do not contain any scenes of an explicit sexual or extremely gross nature. However, there is the very occasional use of bad language, which is sometimes part of the video's humour. The comments sections of many of the clips often contain unnecessarily offensive, puerile and abusive language. They rarely feature any remarks of value and are generally worth switching off or ignoring.

DON'T TRY THIS AT HOME

Some of the book's clips feature stunts performed either by professionals or under the supervision of professionals. Accordingly, the publishers must insist that no one attempt to re-create or re-enact any stunt or activity performed on the featured videos.

HOW TO VIEW THE CLIPS

Each entry is accompanied by a QR code, which you can scan with your iPad or iPod. Alternatively, there is a short URL address, which you can type into your own computer, tablet or phone. Unfortunately, many of the clips are preceded by adverts, these can often be skipped after a few seconds or you may wish to download a reputable advert blocker to prevent them appearing.

CONTENTS

"Time spent with cats is never wasted."

Attributed to Sigmund Freud

THE
MOST AMAZING
YouTube
CAT
VIDEOS EVER!

INTRODUCING GRUMPY CAT

Where it all began for this feline superstar

Morristown, Arizona has a population of just 227, but it is also home to the biggest cat celebrity of them all, Tardar Sauce — better known as Grumpy Cat. With his distinctive hangdog expression (actually the result of a feline form of dwarfism), Tardar Sauce has captured the imagination of YouTube fans across the world. The subject of countless internet memes, a bestselling book (debuting at Number 8 in the *New York Times* non-fiction charts!) and even a feature film, this moggy's popularity shows no sign of slowing down. Just don't expect him to look happy about it.

http://y2u.be/INscMGmhmX4

THE VERY FIRST YOUTUBE CAT VIDEO

A historic post from the early days of the video-sharing platform

There's nothing very memorable about this 30-second clip of a cat called Pajamas jumping for a toy to the strains of 1970's singer-songwriter Nick Drake. However, the "steve" who shared the video is none other than Stephen Chen, one of the three co-founders of YouTube. It was the 26th video to be posted to the site and the very first cat video. Today, it is estimated that there are more than two million cat videos on the site. Between them they have racked up a mind-boggling 24.6 billion views. Here is where it all began.

http://y2u.be/PvTmxDBxtLs

Leabharlanna Poiblí Chathair Bhaile Átha Cliath
Dublin City Public Libraries

CHARLIE SCHMIDT'S KEYBOARD CAT

Vintage VHS footage brings YouTube success

In 1984, Charlie Schmidt filmed his orange tabby cat, Fatso, giving a virtuoso performance on an electric keyboard. He could hardly have imagined that more than 30 years later, his film would have amassed nearly 40 million views on a video-sharing site launched in 2005. In the grainy 1980s footage, Fatso hammers the keyboard keys with feeling (though if you look closely you can see Schmidt's arms controlling the movement beneath the cat's blue shirt). Sadly, Fatso didn't live to see his success. He died in 1987, but the Keyboard Cat phenomenon lives on.

http://y2u.be/J---aiyznGQ

SHOCK AND AWE

The original "surprised kitty"

Is there anything cuter than a kitten throwing its tiny paws in the air while being tickled? In October 2009, this 17-second clip went viral with astonishing speed, collecting more than seven million views in just two weeks. Surprised Kitty's real name is Allila Fluff — Attila after the fearsome warrior and leader of the Huns, Fluff because she is so unbearably cute! To this day, it remains the only video published by Canadian YouTuber rozzafly. It's impossible to top — simply the perfect example of what makes cat videos so compelling to watch.

http://y2u.be/0Bmhjf0rKe8

OMG CAT

Plea for veterinary advice brings internet fame

Chocolate was actually suffering from a dislocated jaw when this video was shot. Her owner uploaded the film in the hope that viewers could advise on suitable treatment, but Chocolate's mouth-wide-open expression made a much bigger splash. Quickly dubbed "OMG cat", Chocolate features in countless mash-ups and videos calling for a suitably stunned feline response. During his takeover of MTV's *Funny or Die* programme in 2010, pop superstar Justin Bieber even spoofed the now very, very viral phenomenon – showing just how far OMG cat had become. Thankfully, though, Chocolate did receive the treatment she needed and made a full recovery.

http://y2u.be/sPmq_4IOmfo

BED WARS

Dogs try to get territorial in the home – with limited success

---

The world is divided into two types of people – cat people and dog people. When asked to describe why they are in the cat camp, people often cite the fact that cats are cool, don't try too hard and are always at least one step ahead of their canine counterparts. This video shows that theory in action as, time after time, dogs of all shapes and sizes do their utmost to evict feline interlopers. Despite spirited efforts, these cats are not going anywhere. It ends with a series of contented pets happy together – even then, though, there's no doubting who's in charge.

http://y2u.be/ovWqEtVVUFs

YOU SHALL NOT PASS

"It's just a cat, dude, come on!"

Another compilation showing the sometimes uneasy relationship that exists between cats and dogs. Again and again, as a dog tries to get where it's going, its path is blocked by an unlikely foe – the family cat. At the bottom of the stairs, in the hallway staring longingly at the promised land beyond – wherever they are, these dogs all seem afraid of the cat impassively staring them down. Complete with comically tentative steps and increasingly desperate efforts from owners to cajole their canines into working up the courage to move forward, this video makes it clear where the power really lies.

http://y2u.be/S7znl_Kpzbs

MEET MARU THE BOX CAT

Big in Japan – and on YouTube

This five-minute introduction to the round-faced, white-socked Scottish Fold from Japan, establishes Maru's playful character, but it's the last 60 seconds that introduces us to what defines him – this is a cat who makes it clear, "I love a box!!" Maru the box cat (as he's now known) is a genuine YouTube superstar. At the time of writing, Maru's homespun videos have received a staggering 282 million views and nearly half a million people subscribe to the channel dedicated to his exploits. Fans all over the world just can't get enough of Maru – and his adorable fascination with sliding around in cardboard boxes.

http://y2u.be/z_AbfPXTKms

TALKING CATS

Contented cats chat about old times

Stina and Mossy are old friends. They get together now and again for a chat, to reminisce about days gone by, when they were kittens and the whole world lay before them. Conversation flows freely and they say a long goodbye with a period of affectionate licking. As the encounter ends, they are already looking forward to their next meeting. Well, that's one interpretation of the original YouTube "talking cats" chat. Many have tried to put their own spin on the conversation, but this remains one of the sweetest examples of the genre.

http://y2u.be/z3U0udLH974

TALKING CATS – A TRANSLATION

Successful spin-off also achieves YouTube success

Nearly five months after the original conversation between two talking cats sent YouTube into a frenzy, this translation offered up one interpretation of what was really going on between Stina and Mossy. It's a droll yet gentle take on the dynamic that could very well be established between two cats who have lived in the same home for a long time. They're grumpy with one another, but any petty squabbles are quickly set to one side as they cleverly conspire when treats are on offer. It's a pretty unflattering portrait of gullible cat owners – but not entirely inaccurate either.

http://y2u.be/1JynBEX_kg8

TAKING THE PLUNGE

Proof that cats don't much like getting wet

There is just a couple of centimetres of water in the bath – it looks inviting, or at the very least intriguing, to this intrepid moggy who inches his way slowly and carefully (complete with a cheeky look to camera) along the side of the tub before taking the plunge – literally. The next few seconds recalls the classic Disney cartoon *Bambi* as our tiny hero slips and slides, paws flying in the air, before finally reaching the safety of the bath edge. It's safe to assume he won't make that mistake again.

http://y2u.be/cR0v4gV5ozU

STANDING CAT

Rocky stands tall like a champion

A 46-second video of a French tabby named Rocky standing
improbably on his hind legs appeared in April 2010. Rocky is
watching something going on outside with great interest, at one
point raising his right paw. The action takes place almost entirely
off screen – but it's the sight of a cat standing straight-backed,
like a human being, combined with the fact that the wobbly
footage is accompanied by a very jaunty anime soundtrack
(Yoko Kanno's "Cats on Mars"), which makes this one of the
strangest and oddly absorbing cat videos in this collection.

http://y2u.be/MVV_HXtEbLo

SIMON'S CAT

**Quirky chronicles of a mischievous cat
running rings around his owner**

When British animator Simon Torfield began the *Simon's Cat*
series in 2008, he can hardly have imagined how successful
it would become. The first episode establishes the tone as the
hungry moggy goes to increasingly comical lengths to wake his
long-suffering owner from a deep sleep. A lot of work goes into
this deceptively simple-looking series – Torfield has said that
each animation usually takes around eight weeks to complete.
What began as a side project, though, quickly proved its worth
as it became an internet smash, and even ran as a regular
feature in a UK tabloid newspaper from 2011 to 2013.

http://y2u.be/w0ffwDYo00Q

KITTEN IN A SPIN

"Trying to make some sense of it all"

Twenty years after its first release, "Stuck in the Middle with You", by Scottish group Stealers Wheel, famously accompanied a gruesome torture scene in Quentin Tarantino's chronicle of a botched heist *Reservoir Dogs*. Fast forward another 20 years and the same song is used as a soundtrack for one of the most endearing cat videos around. Ginger kitten Tom Tom is trying to work out what's going on as he gets himself trapped in a pink hamster ball. The result is two-and-a-half minutes of plaintive tail-grabbing, imploring looks to camera and adorable rolling around. The deadpan reaction of his world-weary playmate is priceless, too.

http://y2u.be/go43XeW6Wg4

CAT RIDES ROOMBA

A very novel way to clean the kitchen

"It's hilarious how normal everything is, except this cat dressed like a shark, riding around the room on a vacuum." One YouTube viewer perfectly sums up the appeal of this cat video classic. Max-Arthur was 14 years old when it was shot and he's completely comfortable in his own fur – happy to wear his shark costume and delighted to board the robotic cleaning machine. Bouncing contentedly off skirting boards and ricocheting gently from the floor cabinets, with his tail swishing merrily behind him, Max-Arthur has clearly taken this ride around the kitchen before.

http://y2u.be/tLt5rBfNucc

A WHOLE NEW WORLD

"I can show you the world – shining, shimmering, splendid"

Here is further proof that cats riding roombas has become a thriving internet cat video sub-genre. Max-Arthur – now better known as Max the roomba cat – stars again in another more imaginative robotic ride released in October 2013. His costume has changed into something a little more elegant, and the roomba has been transformed into a magic carpet as Max-Arthur channels Princess Jasmine in this creative take on Disney's classic *Aladdin*. In the words of the Princess as she is whisked away high into the night sky, this is a cat video that conjures up "indescribable sights, indescribable feelings…"

http://y2u.be/h8UEu5XeDh8

OH! IT'S JUST ME

Horrified reaction to a reflection

YouTube connoisseurs will know that Russia is an especially rich source of cat video content. Cats are considered to bring good luck and anyone moving into to a new home is encouraged to make sure a cat crosses the threshold first to ensure happiness for the household. The creator of this video certainly got lucky when he captured this comic reaction. It looks like the baby is the intended star, but the camera's focus shifts to the left just in time. The addition of the horror movie sound effect works perfectly with this split-second reaction of wide-eyed shock.

http://y2u.be/vZ_YpOvRd3o

CAT MEETS BABY

Oh, OK then... I guess it can stay

The arrival of a new baby can cause disruption in any household — but it's usually the reaction of an elder sibling that concerns parents. In this case, the family pet takes the opportunity to sneak up while a baby's asleep to get a closer look at the strange new creature getting all the attention. What is it? Where did it come from? At the end of the intriguing encounter, it's far from certain that the cat is completely sold on the new addition, but at least that awkward first meeting is out of the way.

http://y2u.be/wHplyDnwwX0

SAYING SORRY

There's more to this apology than you might think

The scene is set with mournful music. Two black and white cats sit – one seems upset, his back turned, facing a wall. Perhaps the other is in the wrong? This theory would seem to be supported by the fact that he gently and repeatedly paws the other on the back. Is this an apology? It certainly looks like one and it seems heartfelt. Surely it will be accepted? Without spoiling the rest of the video, it goes on to prove that cats are incredibly hard to read – it's never safe to assume what's going through the complex feline mind!

http://y2u.be/yNS7zzIzX-E

IS YOUR CAT ACTUALLY A DOG?

Eight signs suggesting the link may be stronger than you think

Cats and dogs are both much-loved domestic animals, but isn't that where the similarities end? This video challenges that assumption, suggesting the two most popular pets on the planet might have more in common that we think. Kodi, a black and white rescue cat, seems to be undergoing a mini identity crisis. He walks on a lead, growls (a bit), pants like a dog, and even appears to listen to his owner's instructions. More than nine million viewers to date have watched his curiously dog-like behaviour – there's even a sequel, the unimaginatively titled, *8 more signs your cat is actually a dog.*

http://y2u.be/OztGJhiBQTo

AN ENGINEER'S GUIDE TO CATS

The science of owning a cat – kind of

Paul Klusman is an aerospace engineer from Wichita, Kansas. He's also a leading player in the cat video world. Back in 2008, Klusman uploaded a video introducing his three cats, Oscar, Ginger and Zoe. It's nearly seven minutes long – an epic in YouTube terms – but its charming low-fi quality really captures the imagination. From the social implications of being a single man with three cats, to the characteristics shared by engineers and their pets, followed by an unexpected and hilarious display of "cat yodelling", this video is real treasure – definitely worth seven minutes of your time.

http://y2u.be/mHXBL6bzAR4

JEDI KITTENS STRIKE BACK

Star Wars + kittens = YouTube gold

A follow-up to the 16-second *Jedi Kittens*, this is a much
more elaborate production from filmmaker Zach King, also
known as FinalCutKing. It's an all-out intergalactic battle,
with starfighters chasing one another through what looks
suspiciously like an office corridor. The dramatic pursuit
comes to a spectacular end when both kittens find themselves
grounded and vulnerable. Only their lightsabers can save them
now. There's time for a brief burst of paw to paw "combat"
before playtime for these two space warriors comes to
a very abrupt (and sweet) conclusion.

http://y2u.be/4Z3r9X8OahA

ONE CONTENTED CAT

Pampering session for one lucky feline

For many, the amount of time spent grooming (and hoovering up afterwards) is one of the definite downsides of cat ownership. Four-year-old BoBo is the exception to the rule. Proving to be the perfect tester for his owner's new vacuum cleaner attachments (a combination floor nozzle and a "crevice" tool in this instance), he just lies back and relaxes while getting his "treatment". Though BoBo simply loves being vacuumed, the filmmakers are keen to point out that not all cats are going to love being "pampered" like this – back to the brush it is, then...

http://y2u.be/C-EZa1OTEYA

THE GAMBLER

Nothing gets past this cool cat

The shell game has its origins in Ancient Greece, but today the "cups and balls" routine is usually seen as a confidence trick – and one you'd be sensible to avoid. In rare cases, though, it can be played honestly and to succeed you need to have some serious skills to carefully follow the ball as it moves. Kido has got the technique well and truly nailed – never taking his eyes off the prize and not letting the addition of a fourth cup throw him off his stride. Sit back and watch him show how it's done.

http://y2u.be/GoXHVs65NFQQ

EPIC FAIL

Wintry conditions get the better of Waffles

Not all YouTube cat videos show their subjects at their super cool, always unruffled and frighteningly intelligent best. Sometimes we get to laugh at their clumsy misadventures too. The wonderfully named Waffles the Terrible certainly presents an excellent opportunity to laugh at misplaced feline confidence. As the large and fluffy ginger cat sizes up the jump before him — from the top of a vehicle covered in snow to an icy garage roof — he's already slipping and sliding ominously. Will he successfully make the leap? You'll just have to watch and find out.

http://y2u.be/5d7aruKYkKs

DANCEFLOOR DREAMS

This kitten does steps in his sleep!

A newborn kitten shows signs of serious dancing talent — while he's asleep. The tiny creature is contentedly napping on his back, snuggling against his mother's belly, when his paws and, eventually, his tail, start to move and tell an utterly bewitching story. The music was a later addition, of course, but more than two million people to date have watched this clip, showing there's definitely an audience out there interested in cat dream interpretation and analysis. And the name of the twinkled-pawed star of the show? Of course, it could only be Twitch!

http://y2u.be/cXeLPYIBFgU

AN UNLIKELY FRIENDSHIP

When Harley (the hedgehog) met Loki (the kitten)

There is no doubt that cats are the undisputed kings when it comes to animals finding fame and gathering views on YouTube. So what do you do if you are trying to come up with a way to introduce your African Pygmy hedgehog to a wider online audience? The answer is simple: borrow your friend's especially charming two-and-a-half-week-old kitten and add a cover version of the tear-jerking Randy Newman song everybody knows from the Pixar classic *Toy Story*. Then just sit back and watch the viewing figures start to climb.

http://y2u.be/D36JUfE1oYk

DIARY OF A SAD CAT

The innermost thoughts of cats everywhere. Maybe.

Owners often say they would love to know what their cat is thinking. Perhaps they should be careful what they wish for if this wildly popular series is anything to go by. Life for these sad cats is full of torment – being stroked with one hand rather than two, the mystery of the water bowl, the indignity of the feeding system… the list goes on. In fact, cats are subject to the every whim of their unseen but omnipotent owners – described in a sinister fashion throughout as "the authorities"– and by the end the viewer is left in no doubt: being a cat is a tough gig.

http://y2u.be/PKffm2ul4dk

Leabharlanna Poiblí Chathair Bhaile Átha Cliath
Dublin City Public Libraries

PRINCE AND DAISY

Affectionate or a bit weird? You decide.

A cat and a sloth star in what is undoubtedly one of the most bizarre cat videos around. It's set to Jason Mraz's Grammy-nominated "I'm Yours", and the end result is either very cute or a little bit creepy. The story of this improbable friendship isn't at all straightforward. Prince's claws feature prominently, but his actions appear to be affectionate. For her part, Daisy doesn't seem too bothered as Prince stokes her face and envelopes her in sloth hugs again and again. At over four minutes, there's plenty of time for you to decide what to make of it all.

http://y2u.be/VACbH_S5ZFo

PAPER FASCINATION

"And yes, I already know – vertical video fail."

Don't shoot your films vertically. It's one of the first rules of YouTube – the fact that this "shot in portrait" video went viral at all is testament to how simple and effective it is. In a nutshell, a cat called Vivey flicks paper repeatedly with her paw. Ignoring her owner's pleas to stop, Vivey continues to pad the paper. It's a gentle study in addictive behaviour – Vivey is completely fixated – and it's surprisingly soothing to watch. As one commenter says, "You know it's been a week when this holds your attention (and makes you giggle) for a full minute and seventeen seconds."

http://y2u.be/jsCLxfFd6KU35

THE MEAN KITTY SONG

Eighty million views and counting

YouTube personality Cory Williams' stats are impressive. At the time of writing, his "smpfilms" channel has more than 600,000 subscribers and over 239 million total views. By far and away his most successful release to date is "The Mean Kitty Song" – a reflection on Williams' first two months with his irascible new kitten, Sparta. All cat owners will recognize something from their own early experiences in this incredibly catchy ditty on what it's like to have your life turned upside down. Released way back in 2007, this charming tribute is still well worth a watch all these years later.

http://y2u.be/Qit3ALTelOo

WHEN CATS ATTACK

**Just when you thought it was safe
to go back in the garden...**

John Williams won an Oscar for his score for the 1975 smash hit
Jaws. The composer himself described the simple, but terrifying,
two note shark theme as a piece of music "grinding away at you,
just as a shark would do, instinctual, relentless, unstoppable."
Here the scene is not Amity Island, but a lush green garden in the
northwest of England. The predator is not a great white shark,
but a grey and white domestic cat. However, the feeling
of suspense and dread is just the same. Or is it?

http://y2u.be/tcxhOGyrCtl

A WINNING FORMULA

YouTube viral video expert shows how it's done

Kevin Nalts is a successful YouTube comedian with a formidable record of creating viral video storms. At the time of writing, his four channels have more than 286 million views. And his single most popular production? Of course, it contains kittens! More than 46 million people have watched *I are cute kitten*, his 2008 step-by-step guide to making a cat video that will appeal to the masses. Keep it short – this one is only 90 seconds long. Maintain the cute – it doesn't stop in this video. Make the animal the star – Nalts even writes the YouTube description in the kitten's "voice". It's simple, but very effective.

http://y2u.be/_ZSbC09qgLl

AN EVOLUTIONARY TALE

Shared traits of the cat family

Anyone who has seen their fair share of nature documentaries will know that big cats are stealthy creatures. The ability of lions, leopards and cheetahs to move silently, and at great speed, across wide open grassland, helps these daylight hunters catch their prey. Domestic cats share the same capacity to spring quickly and escape detection, a fact captured in this perfect 90-second video from Japan. Taking advantage of the disappearance of the camera, this moggy displays perfect poise and ninja skills to creep closer. The sight of his little face up close at the end is a lot more welcoming than the open jaws of his bigger relations!

http://y2u.be/fzzjgBAaWZw

IGGY INVESTIGATES AN iPAD

Curious cat displays lust for technology

When Steve Jobs, the late Apple CEO, launched the first generation iPad in 2010, he spoke of how the revolutionary new tablet "creates and defines an entirely new category of devices that will connect users with their apps and content in a much more intimate, intuitive and fun way than ever before." The Apple guru was probably thinking the users would be human. However, it wasn't long before cat owners discovered the iPad could serve as an (expensive) cat toy too. Iggy shows how it's done – swiping right and playing a tune on the magic piano. Developers are now even creating apps specifically with cats in mind...

http://y2u.be/Q9NP-AeKX40

GOING FOR GOLD

Who says cats can't swim?

Another YouTube hit disproving the popular theory that cats
don't like water. This Russian moggy seems to be having an
absolute whale of a time swimming "lengths" of a bathtub
cheered on by two enthusiastic spectators. It's fair to say
he's not the strongest swimmer around – his doggy paddle
technique is more than a little suspect, and he could definitely
shave a valuable few hundredths of a second off those time
splits by improving his turns, but this water-loving cat
wins the gold medal for effort and adorableness.

http://y2u.be/My1K9kC-sQg

PLEASE DON'T GO

Kitten with serious separation issues

Some people think cats tend towards being loners – ignoring
their owners and generally happy to do their own thing so long
as tasty food appears regularly. However, some just can't bear
to be parted from their loved ones – even for a moment. This
Russian kitten is extraordinarily clingy, going to great lengths
to stop the object of its affection leaving for work. Needy?
Yes. Annoying? Potentially, especially if it happens every day.
But the imploring look flashed right at the end – amplified
by the mournful soundtrack – means you would need
a heart of stone to stay angry for long.

http://y2u.be/xVy_XII3wSI

VINYL CAT

Reggae-loving moggy on the decks

With so many YouTube cat videos available these days, it's getting harder and harder to produce one that stands out from the crowd. While some aim for higher production values, and even higher concepts, this exquisitely simple example captures just what it is that makes the genre so popular – the unpredictable nature of cats. Just 52 seconds long, it features two-year-old Furby, one turntable and the voice of Bob Marley. Watch as Furby gets to grips with the classics – "Is this Love?" and "Three Little Birds" – then see what's really piqued his interest.

http://y2u.be/K7dcSr04G8s

NONONONO CAT

Cat video fans say "yes"

Marquis, a domestic Siberian cat, is not at all happy to have strangers in his home. His reaction is nervous, rather than aggressive, but also sounds uncannily like a human saying "no" on loop. Back in 2011, Marquis' distinctive "talent" was viewed over 500,000 times in a single day and it has also inspired a huge number of inventive responses – a search for "NoNoNoNo cat remix" on YouTube returns more than 8,000 results! There are the obvious riffs on Amy Winehouse and Destiny's Child, but Marquis has also been the subject of one of YouTube's most enduring memes – a Hitler *Downfall* parody.

http://y2u.be/oKI-tDOL18A

LETTING A DOG TAKE THE STRAIN

An unusual way of catching a lift home

Chihuahuas may be small, but the breed is known for being quick, courageous and fiercely loyal. Responding to off-camera encouragement — YouTube reliably informs us that the Russian-speaking woman is giving the instruction to "carry her home, dog" — this tiny dog rescues the kitten from a ledge and gives it a fireman's lift-style ride back to the safety of the house. There are a couple of pit stops along the way, and it doesn't look like the most comfortable of journeys, but both parties seem perfectly fine with it. A heartwarming show of devotion.

http://y2u.be/9L8MvMBZ1nU

ONE PERSISTENT PARROT

Brave (or foolish) bird keeps coming back for more

Sitting imperiously on top of a sofa, this spectacularly furry ginger cat thinks he's got it all worked out. He clearly hadn't reckoned with a persistent parrot swooping in to disturb his well-earned peace. He swats his chirping nemesis away repeatedly, but the bird keeps on returning and getting right up in this Garfield lookalike's grill. His thoroughly fed-up expression at the close is unmissable – this is a cat with a grouchy look to camera that could give Tardar Sauce a real run for his money when it comes to feline grumpiness.

http://y2u.be/9qL-MD53qDs

NYAN CAT

YouTube fame lies at the end of this rainbow

Chris Torres' Russian Blue cat, Marly, named after *Back to the Future* hero Marty McFly, was the inspiration behind Nyan or "pop tart cat". The Texas-based illustrator's smash hit began life as an 8-bit animated GIF, but the pixel picture of a cat with the body of a pop tart flying through the sky really took off once it was paired with an infectious Japanese synth-pop loop. Marly died in 2012, but Nyan lives on. His is a YouTube success story of many twists and turns — copyright wrangles, lawsuits and countless spin-offs. But the original keeps on going strong and has over 118 million views to date.

http://y2u.be/QH2-TGUlwu4

THE RESCUE

Heroic rescue has a heartbreaking ending

California firefighter Cory Kalanick was checking through the ruins of a home destroyed by fire when he spotted the lifeless body of a kitten on the floor. Thirty minutes later, through a combination of oxygen from a child-sized mask and heart massage, Lucky was revived. The unfolding story was captured on Kalanick's helmet camera and used to create *The Rescue* – produced in the style of a Hollywood trailer. Sadly, Lucky's lungs were too badly damaged to survive and he died just hours later. However, the dramatic story helped raise the profile of emergency veterinary medicine and raised a lot of money for the cause.

hhttp://y2u.be/5fVusgCVkPg

HAMMOCK TIME

Timo's persistence eventually pays off

When Timo's owners gave him his very own cat-sized hammock
to lounge in, they probably didn't think his efforts to get to grips
with the new toy would provide material fit for a YouTube trilogy. It
is hard to look elegant when getting into a hammock, and it can
take a little time to master the technique without flipping straight
back out – but it took this shaggy ragdoll four long months to get
it right. His experiments with various different methods of getting
(and staying) in show true dedication to the pursuit of total
relaxation. Thankfully, it all works out in the end.

http://y2u.be/c4U_z7v0Vl4

AN OFFICER AND A KITTEN

Kitten can't get in the way of a speeding ticket

A policeman making a routine traffic stop in Taylor, Texas, encounters a kitten that just demands attention — and it was all caught on camera from the patrol car. As Keith Urban tries to issue a speeding ticket, a black kitten darts into view and starts to climb all over the officer, eventually making it to the top of his head. It wasn't a cunning ruse from the driver about to receive his penalty, though — the daring kitten comes out of nowhere — and Officer Urban keeps his concentration firmly on the job in hand, staying calm and professional before sending the driver on his way.

http://y2u.be/i_zRPWyATZw

THE ANFIELD CAT

"How on earth does a cat get into a football stadium?"

With both teams chasing Champions League qualification, the stakes were high when Spurs travelled to Anfield in Februrary 2012. The game is best remembered not for the skills on show from players like Luka Modric or Gareth Bale, or the return of Luis Suárez after suspension, but instead for the appearance of a cat on the pitch. The stray tabby was apparently a familiar face around the Liverpool ground, but had never before got so close to the action. The unexpected Anfield cat cameo certainly provided more entertainment than the supposed superstars on the pitch – the game ended goalless.

http://y2u.be/NKQQxXA6Cic

CANNES, BERLIN, LONDON... MINNEAPOLIS

Meet the very first winner of the coveted People's Choice award

---

When Katie Hill came up with the idea of an Internet Cat Video Festival in 2012, she wasn't expecting her employer to take her up on it. After all, the Walker Art Center in Minneapolis is one of America's foremost modern art galleries. Yet the phenomenon was now too big to ignore and more than 10,000 people flocked to see cat videos grouped by category. Visitors to the Walker website were able to get involved as well by voting for their favourite. The winner of the inaugural Golden Kitty award was this two-minute, Gallic-infused study of the existential angst of a house cat.

http://y2u.be/Q34z5dCmC4M

HENRI VISITS THE VET

"They pronounce me healthy, as always"

Henri le chat noir is the brainchild of Will Braden, a Seattle-based filmmaker. His auteur-style videos, in French with English subtitles, offer a glimpse into Henri's inner soul as he endures the torture of everyday life. Predictably, a visit to the vet does little to lift the depressive Henri's spirits. He is tormented by "growing disillusionment with the world", suspicious of the intentions of his "caretakers", and even the news of his new-found internet fame after his Golden Kitty triumph doesn't brighten Henri's mood. Braden really hit on a winning formula when he created this avant-garde YouTube sensation.

http://y2u.be/liYUzYozsAQ

WHO'S REALLY IN CHARGE?

An interesting interpretation of the dynamic between a cat and its owner

Ever wondered what's really going on in your cat's head? Global internet news company BuzzFeed offers some answers in this funny short. Though the company has expanded to become a more serious news-driven organization, it still provides a wealth of viral content alongside its hard-hitting political scoops. And cat videos are very popular indeed with BuzzFeed's growing audience. You can even sign up to receive a dedicated Week in Cats e-mail newsletter. This original animation is firmly tongue-in-cheek, but some cat owners may suspect this interpretation is not too far off the mark.

http://y2u.be/TPJWuImLbtc

SIBLINGS IN SYNC

Dancing chorus line of kittens

The exploits of five Scottish Fold kittens — Rocky, Raoul, Rosie, Ruby and Rio — can't fail to raise a smile. There's something pleasingly unpolished about this video: it's not hard to see what's mesmerizing the Fab Five, but it's the small un-choreographed details that have made this routine so popular. The way in which the kitten second on the left with the white belly is so much more easily distracted than his siblings, often just a beat out of time, or even not following the movement at all. Look out for the distinctive folded ears of the kitten on the far right too!

http://y2u.be/pLCOTpjBGcs

A CHALLENGING INTRODUCTION

Brave kitten stands up to a fierce-looking dog

As introductions go, this is pretty tense, but the courage of this plucky kitten is impressive. The dog is looking to play and at no point does it seem like the kitten is in imminent danger – in this case, it's true that the Rottweiler's bark is far worse than its (non-existent) bite. But the sheer difference in size means it's not the most comfortable watch – though the kitten's gutsy attempts to charge the much larger animal are definitely noteworthy. It may have more than 43 million views to date, but this video has divided more fans than most.

http://y2u.be/DNeaZz9Vt6Q

THE BATTLE OF THE BOX

Sibling rivalry threatens to spill over

Proof that cats have loved boxes long before Maru the box cat
came on the scene. An oldie from 2006, this is a classic study
in sibling jealousy and the triumph of strength and willpower.
Sibling squabbles often have their roots in territorial disputes. In
this case, the territory is a cardboard tissue box – one kitten is
safely (and very sweetly) ensconced inside, the other two want in.
The relaxing music is a little incongruous given how much effort
is expended as all three try to achieve their desired outcome.
Watch to see which one comes out on top.

http://y2u.be/vdQj2ohqCBk

KITTENS AT LUNCH

Persian kittens learning to chow down

Persian cats have often got a raw deal in popular culture. Think of
Duchess, the spoiled villain of the film *Babe*, and the trademark
white cat belonging to legendary Bond villain Ernst Stavro Blofeld.
Here, though, the long-haired breed gets some overdue positive
coverage with a choreographed display of round-faced cuteness.
Crafty camera work and clever angles, teamed with a rousing
Russian soundtrack that works perfectly with the footage, make
this video a definite hit. The kittens were just two months old
when this video was filmed – I wonder where they are now.

http://y2u.be/wNv74rvkAw8

KITTEN CONFUSED BY A WATERMELON

Summary superfood sends this kitten crazy

Four-month-old Flanigan is clearly spooked by his encounter with a watermelon. After a thorough investigation, and several attempts to manoeuvre himself underneath the fruit, he's still none the wiser about the giant green sphere and makes a bolt for the exit. It doesn't look like a particularly vicious confrontation, but Flanigan's owner confirms that the watermelon came off worse, "[it] had scratches and bite marks all over it by the time kitty was done. Flanigan walked away from the battle unscathed. He's a funny cat." More than 19 million people appear to agree.

http://y2u.be/0vmoZEaN_-o

COOPER LOVES WATERMELON

But sharing is definitely off the menu

Cats can be notoriously fickle eaters, often refusing to eat anything but a specific brand of food. If you were to make a list of all their favourite treats, it's unlikely that watermelon would feature. But Cooper has worked out what lies beneath the tough green skin and just can't get enough of the refreshing summer fruit. The fabulously fluffy Persian loves watermelon so much that he's not prepared to share his slice. When a couple of dogs try to get in on the action, Cooper is quick to shut them down.

http://y2u.be/i3cHNObcEh8

ON THE WOBBLY ROAD TO RECOVERY

Kitten still sedated after a visit to the vet

Many people describe sedation as an experience that leaves them feeling happy, calm, relaxed, a little groggy – and maybe even just a little bit drunk. This super cute kitten, recovering from a minor procedure, displays all the textbook signs of having recently "gone under". It's drowsy and disorientated, unsteady on its paws, and would definitely have trouble walking in a straight line. The side effects are only temporary – but the woozy way this kitten is bouncing back to health, complete with dozy and lingering looks to camera, is especially delightful.

http://y2u.be/aA3dHi_o7Yw

DIVINE INTERVENTION

"Dear Lord, please forgive me..."

Billy was 18 years old when this video was made. He'd lived a long, full and happy life, with no major regrets. He just happened to like to fall asleep in a strange position, with his head bowed as though deep in prayer. Head pressed firmly down, he confesses his "sins" and pleads for absolution. However, as his long litany of crimes and misdemeanors is recounted, it's hard to be certain that Billy's show of spirituality and devotion is all it's cracked up to be. Make sure you watch this one all the way to the end.

http://y2u.be/-ltqz3EpufU

PLAY IT AGAIN, NORA!

Piano-playing prodigy takes a turn

Adopted as a kitten from a New Jersey animal shelter, Nora was
a year old when the first signs of her prodigious musical talent
began to show. After observing her piano teacher owner deliver
lessons, Nora started to play. This is her debut performance.
The sequel – a much more richly produced film – has received
much more attention on YouTube, but this 90-second version
is a perfect introduction to Nora's very individual style. Since
Nora first hit the headlines in 2007, she has fascinated animal
behaviour experts and continued to expand her repertoire – even
performing duets with her owner. An unlikely musical maestro.

http://y2u.be/5fGQLHKx-Y00

Leabharlanna Poibli Chathair Bhaile Átha Cliath
Dublin City Public Libraries

YELLING CAT

Communication breakdown in Brooklyn

It's frustrating when no matter how hard you try, you just can't seem to make yourself understood. If faced with this situation, it's important to remain calm and considered and not to lose your temper. It's a life lesson this Brooklyn-based moggy still needs to learn because he quickly lets his irritation get the better of him. The increasingly shrill attempts of this "talking cat" to get a message across to his owner definitely don't have the desired effect. Particularly vocal, letting out a serious hiss and even swatting the door to emphasize a point, this cat gets *LOUD*.

http://y2u.be/Yie9Bgo69m8

TIGGER SAYS NO

Definitely not a fan of bath time

For every YouTube video proclaiming that cats actually *do* love water, there's another showing exactly the opposite. Tigger reverts to type with a full-on freak out as he's given his first bath. There's no doubting what he thinks about it, but the experience leaves no lasting scars. As his owner says, "We decided to film it because as soon as I started running the water, Tigger started making funny odd noises we had never heard, so we just thought maybe we should capture it! He is perfectly fine and was back to his usual self 5 minutes after the bath. No harm done!"

http://y2u.be/PM5BCjNswd0

BREAKING UP A FIGHT

Playing the peacemaker in an unusual fashion

Two kittens are embroiled in a play fight that's full of claws and attitude. They are soon joined by a third, who watches from a short distance before coming up with an extremely novel way of calming things down. Without spoiling the surprise, the peacemaker's unorthodox technique does succeed in distracting the scrapping siblings, but perhaps the most comical part of this 2007 hit is the direction (or lack of it) of the intervention. Many cat owners will empathize with the owner who has to deal with the mess a kitten can leave behind.

http://y2u.be/YLDbGqJ2KYk

CAT VERSUS PRINTER

Paper jam! Please load paper! Paper jam!

Home printers get a very bad press. We can just about tolerate their idiosyncratic ways in an office, but at home it can be a real battle. At their worst, printers make technophobes of us all. Cat versus printer videos have been around for a while, as enterprising YouTubers found that the machine's mysterious beeps and frequent malfunctions can prompt a funny feline reaction. Complete with arcade game-style sound effects, this is probably the best. It captures exactly the anger and frustration many of us feel when faced once again with an inexplicable paper jam.

http://y2u.be/REQRHdMRimw

A MOTHER'S LOVE

Approach with caution: extremely cute

The title says it all. A 60-second delight, this was declared the cutest cat video on the internet when it first appeared in May 2011. Refreshingly simple, without background music and made up entirely of wobbly handheld footage, it shows a mother comforting her sleeping kitten, pulling it closer as the youngster seems agitated, perhaps by a dream. Proving we just can't get enough of enchanting cats on camera, its popularity has endured and, at the time of writing, more than 57 million people have checked it out. A definite YouTube classic.

http://y2u.be/Vw4KVoEVcr0

FOLLOW MY LEAD

Mother shows her baby the way

Parents set out to teach their children by example and it seems cats follow the same parenting principle. An adventurous kitten learns valuable life lessons about tree climbing, the dangers of overconfidence and how to get himself out a potentially sticky situation – all with a little help and gentle encouragement from his mother. The video's original title, *Mama Kitty's Rescue* is a bit misleading. It's not a dramatic high-octane recovery operation – rather, a patient, two-minute tutorial with a surprising and rewarding conclusion. It seems kittens need role models too.

http://y2u.be/RkJEwYfz68o

A VERY ANGRY CAT

Don't you dare come any closer!

YouTube is full of angry cats. Sometimes the videos can be tough to watch, especially when it's not clear why the animals are behaving as they are. Of course, some cats are just bad-tempered – and woe betide anyone who tries to get them to do something against their will. The set-up here is like a sitcom: a black cat glowers and hisses from its comfortable bed while close by, another purrs contentedly, full of warmth and affection. The contrast between the two could not be clearer. The canine visitor at the close doesn't know what to make of it all either.

http://y2u.be/hcr7cszxlNk

FROZEN – KITTEN VERSION

"The cold never bothered me anyway"

The Pet Collective describes itself as the "ultimate destination for pet lovers on the internet". From tear-jerking and inspirational vignettes to 24/7 live streams of just-born litters of puppies and kittens, it's proved terrifically popular, with over half a million YouTube subscribers. It's also garnered a reputation for some of the most imaginative and well-executed popular culture pet parodies. The Collective's version of Disney's 2013 blockbuster *Frozen* is a prime example. A feline remake of the most commercially successful animated film ever was sure to be a winner. As one commentator proclaimed after watching, "I die of fluffiness!"

http://y2u.be/0mmGI3jLDfU

TEN DAYS APART

A very, very emotional reunion

Working out the ratio of cat years to human years is not an exact science. Experts tend to concur that the first 24 months of a cat's life is roughly equivalent to the first 25 years of a human's lifespan. It's safe to assume that Jaspar, the excitable star of this video, has yet to reach the two-year milestone. He has only been parted from his beloved canine companion for 10 days, but it obviously felt like an eternity. Jaspar's wholehearted burst of affection, coupled with Bow-Z the dog's winning stoicism, makes this reunion impossible not to like.

http://y2u.be/HvXMVDOhgJ4

DRAMATIC CAT

Hitchcockian homage to a "chipmunk"

Five years before the launch of Vine, the seven-second video-sharing service, the success of a five-second video called *Dramatic chipmunk* had already signalled that short and funny was the way to go. The quick-fire footage, taken from a Japanese TV show, showed a "chipmunk" (actually a prairie dog), turning to face the camera accompanied by a burst of ominous orchestral music. The same audio, taken from the 1974 film *Young Frankenstein*, features in the cat video homage. The camera angle doesn't quite recall Hitchcock in the same manner as the original, but it's still a worthy tribute – and only 21 seconds long.

http://y2u.be/plWnm7UpsXk

DANCE, DANCE, DANCE...

A tune that's almost guaranteed to get stuck in your head. Sorry.

A real old school classic from 2004, this one predates YouTube itself. Steve Ibsen created the video from old photos of his cat Kayla and used stop motion animation software to inject her with some rhythm, making it appear as though she is dancing. Fast forward 11 years and Ibsen's catchy creation is still going strong, even if production values have come on a little in the intervening period. Be warned – once you've heard the Kitty Cat Dance, it's almost impossible to unhear it. Altogether now – "CAT, I'm a kitty cat, and I dance, dance, dance..."

http://y2u.be/SaA_cs4WZHM

WITHERING HEIGHTS

"Why are you so disgusted?"

There's something about pets with traditionally human names.
The sound of an owner calling after a dog running off the lead
with cries of "Tony! Tony!" or the escapades of a cat called
"Dave" just can't fail to raise a smile. It's just very hard to take
this magnificently named moggy seriously. With a supreme line
in disdainful looks, Gary is definitely *not* impressed by what's
going on beneath him. As he surveys his kingdom from
a lofty perch, we're left in no doubt as to the object
of Gary's scorn. Not that Pedro seems to care.

http://y2u.be/4NEwCp9AyYg

LES CHATS NINJAS

Clever compilation of cats and their unexpected ninja moves

French cinema has a long and rich history. The New Wave of the late 1950s and early 1960s revolutionized the art of filmmaking and the stars of the movement – including Jean-Luc Godard, François Truffaut and Claude Chabrol – are still feted today. It's only right then, that the world's foremost celebration of the Ninja Cat phenomenon should come from the home of European cinema. OK – so it's a not-very-sophisticated collection of clips from all over the internet showing cats at their stealthy, acrobatic best. Yet, the addition of a French narrator elevates the whole thing to much greater heights.

http://y2u.be/HBfy_kjkt4I

BANANAS ABOUT BANANAS

It could be difficult to get five-a-day when Winston's about

Blogger Rich Juzwiak found the cat of his dreams in Winston.
"Growing up in the 1980s, there were so many fuzzy, impossible,
mythic creatures to covet: mogwai, Gurgi, various Muppets,
things that I wanted so bad. With Winston, I finally got my
mogwai." There's no doubt Winston's unique look helped him
become a YouTube star, but it was his love of bananas – or more
specifically, his love of keeping them safely out of the way of
dangerous human hands – that really made his name.
Winston is a cat who takes fruit security very, very seriously.

http://y2u.be/xPZ7G3H-pwU

"SERENGETI BLISS"

Watching a kitten shouldn't be this relaxing

A video of an ordinary kitten playing on an ordinary day in an
ordinary garden becomes so much more than the sum of its parts
with the addition of an uplifting soundtrack and the use of a
slow-motion camera. The song is actually titled "Serengeti Bliss",
and it's not hard to imagine an East African setting taking the
place of the domestic garden. In fact, this video is
an advertisement for the camera in question and, while
it definitely does a good job in showing off what it can do,
most people will probably just remember the cute kitten…

http://y2u.be/J1vpB6h3ek4

DON'T WORRY, GUYS, I'VE GOT THIS

Cat displays astonishing baby whispering powers

The internet is awash with theories, advice and countless "sleep strategies" for parents looking to find out how to get their babies to stop crying and drift off peacefully. It's unlikely that the technique practised by Stewie on a grouchy and agitated baby boy in Canada would feature very highly on sleep experts' list of recommended remedies, but it definitely seems to work. Stewie is in complete control of the situation from start to finish. Make sure you watch this one all the way through – Stewie's expression at the very end says simply, "This is how it's done."

http://y2u.be/PWXigjFm4TM

BORN TO BE CARRIED

"He is the biggest baby of a cat"

From a cat that can soothe a crying baby to sleep to one that thinks it is a baby. Three-year-old Garfield just loves to be carried and his default position is at his owner's feet begging to be taken into his arms. Alex Amaral says he decided to shoot the short "as a bit of a response to all the people out there who claim that cats are incapable of showing any kind of affection or bonding with humans. My little guy is always at my side and he is the biggest baby of a cat." Having watched Garfield in action, you'll find it hard to argue.

http://y2u.be/Meol5agN5DQ

KEYBOARD WARRIORS

Why are cats so attracted to laptops?

Cats love laptops. There is even a Twitter feed that retweets pictures from would-be workers all over the world whose efforts are being thwarted by an immovable feline. There are several explanations for this problem that's very much of the 21st century. Cats like to lounge where it's warm. If the sun isn't shining outside, they can recreate the tropical vibe simply by lying on top of a keyboard. They are also willing to fight for attention. So, if a cat thinks its owner is spending too much time staring at a screen, then that's where the battle lines are drawn.

http://y2u.be/UMerTU8Z5zI

A VERY POLITE CAT

A cat who knows how to say "please"

Proving it *is* possible to train a cat to have good manners, this family pet is unfailingly polite when it comes to asking for affection. And the respectful approach pays off handsomely. This is a cat who knows exactly what it wants, and exactly how to go about getting it. But it's also a video about setting boundaries. One to watch for every owner out there who is tired of feeling like their pet is in charge — and sick of removing cat hair from their sofa. This is either going to inspire you or be the cause of deep, deep frustration!

http://y2u.be/zQS0DsfGLYc

BABY'S BEST FRIEND

The start of a beautiful friendship?

A 60-second study in cute, this is a kid who seriously loves his pet. And while the shower of affection seems a little one-sided, it's not every cat that would put up with her cosy bed being infiltrated, a series of smothering hugs from an eager toddler and some over-enthusiastic petting. Sadie doesn't look entirely onamoured of the situation she's found herself in – the glazed stare into the middle-distance is a giveaway – but she'll patiently put up with it for now. She's even helping to teach the child to talk – let's hope "Sadie" wasn't his first word!

http://y2u.be/Vweh3hWrInM

PEANUT'S STORY MAKES THE PAPER

Baby squirrel nursed alongside litter of kittens

Founded in 1877, the *Washington Post* is known for its hard-hitting coverage of the US political scene – what's going on in the White House and on Capitol Hill. It broke the Watergate story that led to President Nixon's resignation and has won 47 Pulitzer Prizes. Even the *Washington Post* likes cat videos. Its 2014 story of Peanut, an orphaned squirrel saved by a compassionate cat who nursed the tiny creature alongside her own litter, melted hearts. As the *Post* said, "There are few things cuter than kittens, except maybe for baby squirrels. Put those together and it's like a furry Reese's Peanut Butter Cup."

http://y2u.be/jKlv1EtHj08

LIL BUB RESTING BY AN OPEN FIRE

Superstar cat makes atmospheric festive appearance

These days the biggest cat celebrities are successful across social media platforms. Lil Bub has a thriving presence on Instagram, Facebook and Twitter as well as YouTube. The runt of a litter, she was rescued from a shelter and has overcome a series of health challenges, including osteoporosis, which restricts her movements. Her distinctive look – almost permanently kitten-like – is the result of a number of genetic mutations. Video isn't her natural medium, but that didn't stop this *hour*-long special becoming a soothing festive hit.

http://y2u.be/ZuHZSbPJhaY

ALLIGATOR BLINKS FIRST

**Swamp standoff as alligators come
face to face with a surprising foe**

Pet Cat Saves Boy from Two Vicious GATORS. Clever YouTube
titles drive traffic, creating a sense of drama or suspense to
entice viewers to click through to the action. In this case, the
original title is not very accurate because at no point is the
child ever really in danger. However, this cat scares off not one
but two alligators. Faced with a regular and otherwise perfectly
friendly cat who is receptive to human affection, they can't
get back to the safety of the Louisiana swamps quick enough.
That in itself is pretty remarkable to watch.

http://y2u.be/5sAF8gMN9c0

MUM TO THE RESCUE

There's no time to mess around when a kitten's in danger

An already delicate recovery operation takes a sudden turn for
the worse in this Russian rescue video. From the angle at which
the film is recorded, it's not immediately clear why the situation
is so perilous, and the mother's initial rescue attempts to reach
her kitten are a little half-hearted. The difference between
these first tentative steps and the lightning speed of her
reactions at the end is startling. With her kitten in real trouble,
she's not moving gingerly now. A heartwarming illustration
of the bond between a mother and her offspring.

http://y2u.be/5sAF8gMN9c0

FIVE STAR REVIEW

Wampa casts a critical eye over new *Star Wars* trailer

A YouTube video of a cat watching YouTube. So far, so meta.
Named after the terrifying creatures who roamed the ice planet
Hoth, Siamese kitten Wampa already has an affinity with the
hugely successful film franchise. And she definitely gives the
critical seal of approval to the trailer for the much-anticipated
Star Wars: Episode VII. Wampa's clearly heavily invested in the
action unfolding onscreen – even if she does seem a little fearful
at one point, pausing to check whether arch villain Darth
Vader is lurking behind the iPad. (Spoiler alert: he's not.)

http://y2u.be/QPdnk-ZEJtU

MOBSTER CAT

**Channelling Francis Ford Coppola's saga
of organized crime and family life**

The first film in the *Godfather* trilogy begins at a wedding party.
Guests queue to see Don Vito Corleone because "no Sicilian
can refuse a request on his daughter's wedding day." While
the atmosphere outside is full of joy, inside it's all about power
and influence, as Brando's Godfather listens to pleas for help,
cradling a tabby cat. OK, so this is just 30 seconds long, and
hasn't racked up very many views, but it's another celebration
with a strong central character. The instantly recognizable
music helps — this cat is the boss of the family too.

http://y2u.be/cETvMaX6vR8

IT'S RAINING CATS

Weatherman keeps his cool as cat creeps onscreen

Eduardo Rodriguez shows remarkable professionalism when his live weather forecast is interrupted by a very unexpected visitor. The veteran meteorologist doesn't miss a beat as the cat makes his entrance, and simply continues to tell the people of Florida about the weather heading their way. The car park of the Miami-based Univision TV station is home to a number of strays — but this was the first time one of them managed to get into the studio and in front of the camera. Live TV has always been a rich source of blooper material and this is a worthy addition to the archive.

http://y2u.be/xCIRsQ7ENsc

OUT FOR THE COUNT

Nothing is going to wake this kitten up

On average, cats sleep for an astonishing 15 hours a day. A very young kitten may spend as much as 90 per cent of their time in the land of nod. The single-minded pursuit of rest and relaxation can be seen in this video, which has clocked up more than three million views to date. Spread-eagled on a computer desk — for once, alongside, rather than on top of a keyboard — this tiny kitten bravely resists all attempts to rouse him from what is obviously a very deep and enjoyable slumber. He's serious about sleeping. Nothing and nobody is going to get in his way.

http://y2u.be/ZCdZtsiOWvo

THE RISE OF COLONEL MEOW

Scowling, scotch drinking and much-missed cat video star

Giving Grumpy Cat a run for his money in the surly stakes, this Himalayan-Persian crossbreed was awarded a Guinness World Record on account of the length of his fur in 2013. (If you're interested, his average hair length was 25 centimetres/ 10 inches!) But, as well as his fur, Colonel Meow was revered for his dramatic scowl and plans for world domination. At least, according to his owner, or self-styled "slave beast", Anne Marie Avey. The Colonel's fans, or "minions" as he preferred to call them, were devastated by his death in 2014, but this skillfully put together record of his "rise to power" is a fitting tribute.

http://y2u.be/RYHcnpfkxqY

WHAT AN ENTRANCE

Nothing can stop this cat from reaching his dinner

A huge winter storm in Quebec, Canada left Ann Got's front
door blocked by a wall of snow. But her cat had seen this kind
of extreme weather before, and Plume certainly wasn't going
to let a simple snow drift disrupt his schedule. As the door
opens, and his owner calls him in for food, there's only one
thing on his mind. At 14 years old, Plume is perhaps a little too
old to be making such a dramatic entrance, but it's definitely
entertaining to watch. He even seems a little surprised
at his own athleticism at the end.

http://y2u.be/MtGog4Cb7RY

HAMILTON'S HIPSTER CREDENTIALS

This cat is too cool for school

With his distinctive and perfectly shaped handlebar mustache, Hamilton — or Hammy — is a relative newcomer to the Cat Pack. Raised in the San Francisco Bay Area, Hammy has a hectic social media life — he's more into the hipster-friendly short-form sharing format, but this YouTube compilation of his greatest Vines just why he has become a star. In 2014, Hammy was diagnosed with a serious congenital hip defect requiring urgent and expensive surgery. His fans quickly came to the rescue, donating more than $6,000 to a crowdfunding campaign set up to cover the costs of treatment.

http://y2u.be/8_AoCxNUyaU

OSCAR'S STORY

An ordinary cat with extraordinary powers

Oscar is one of a number of cats who call the Steere House Nursing and Rehabilitation Center in Providence, Rhode Island home. He lives on the third floor, where patients are suffering from dementia and coming to the end of their lives. In 2007, staff noticed Oscar had a remarkable ability to recognize when a patient was within a few hours of death. Time and again, they watched as he made his way to the dying person's room and stayed with them until they passed away. There is no single explanation for Oscar's appearances, but it's an incredible story.

http://y2u.be/c-R5wdywfZE

LET SLEEPING CATS LIE

How to fall asleep anywhere, anytime

What could be better than watching a soothing video of a cat sleeping? Watching a three-minute compilation of a series of cats sleeping in increasingly improbable positions, that's what. Whether on plant pots or foosball tables, and no matter how contorted and uncomfortable they might look, these happy creatures are dead to the world. As medical evidence on the dangers of sleep loss mounts, with some of the blame falling on increased technology use, maybe cats can teach us humans a thing or two when it comes to their total commitment to catching ZZZs. Watch and learn.

http://y2u.be/vwji6HiXWCs

TARA THE HERO CAT

The hero cat that sees off a vicious dog

Four-year-old Jeremy Triantafilo was happily playing on his bike just outside his home when a neighbour's dog pounced. Within seconds the Triantafilo's tabby Tara leapt into action and saved the little boy. The attack was captured on CCTV and news of Tara's heroism spread quickly. She received plaudits from all over the world and officials from Kern County, California, the scene of the rescue, declared 3 June as "Tara the Hero Cat Day". The footage is dramatic and it's clear the outcome could have been a lot worse had it not been for the rapid and fearless reaction of the family pet.

http://y2u.be/ckDVpihCPq8

A PAIR OF SAFE PAWS

Ginger cat makes a bid to join list of goalkeeping greats

Peter Bonetti made 495 appearances for Chelsea in the 1960s and 1970s. He was known as "the cat of Stamford Bridge", a tribute to his graceful movement and incredible agility. At the same time, Bayern Munich fans also christened their elastic-armed shot stopper, Sepp Maier, "die katze" (the cat). To this list, we can add Sissi, a ginger cat from the Italian city of Brescia, who adores playing football with his owner. Although he displays great reactions and plenty of enthusiasm to pluck the ball from the air, Sissi's talent is perhaps still a little raw.

http://y2u.be/VxjPo1PLrCw

MEET MEREDITH SWIFT

Most famous cat(s) in pop

When a very famous soft drink manufacturer asked pop superstar Taylor Swift what life would be like if it tasted like their popular sugar-free product, she didn't hesitate. Her answer? A room full of kittens! OK, so this was material for a TV advert, but there's no disputing the fact that Swift is cat crazy. She documents the adventures of her faithful feline companions, Meredith and Olivia, across social media and this simple introduction to an attention-seeking Meredith — still a kitten back in 2011 — went down a storm with her adoring fans.

http://y2u.be/ggwKZh6TsNU

CAT CAN'T GET OUT OF THE BAG

The mystery of cats' obsession with plastic

For some reason, cats are fascinated by plastic bags. People have speculated that it could be because of their shiny smooth texture, the distinctive smell, the way the bags make a "crinkly" noise, or even because cats associate them with food. No one really knows exactly *why* cats love them — but they definitely do. For this curious cat the sight of an empty bag on the table was tantalizing, the opportunity to take a closer look just too difficult to ignore. However, he gets a little more than he bargained for, as the bag bites back!

http://y2u.be/CdYZnft3SI8

WITH OR WITHOUT THE MUSIC?

Icelandic pop legend or simple dawn chorus? You decide.

There is a school of thought that the unnecessary addition of a soundtrack can ruin a potentially great video. Viewers begged for a music-free version of this YouTube hit and their wish was eventually granted. You can watch with or without the sound of Bjork – her extraordinary voice makes the strange scene even stranger. (As if the sight of a herd of deer walking in single file down a road wasn't weird enough.) Stripped of the audio track, the encounter is perhaps more menacing and cinematic. Either way, it's another example of cats' refusal to be cowed by creatures much bigger than they are.

http://y2u.be/6NA-ccJ1BpM

A HELPING PAW

What goes up must come down

Six-month-old Bella is obviously nervous about getting down from the attic. But there's only one option available. She sizes up the situation, takes a deep breath and carefully sets off, determined not to rush her descent. Kimba has other ideas and nonchalantly sticks out a paw... It's a quick fire, slapstick hit and Bella suffered no ill effects from her fall, despite the dramatic sound effects. At just 11 seconds long, this is a viral favourite to enjoy again and again. Even though you might feel a little bit guilty for finding Bella's tumble amusing.

http://y2u.be/V3GJycgu-cs

KITTEN WITH SUPERPOWERS

The pig doesn't stand a chance

You don't often see pigs and kittens together — especially not in what looks like a domestic living room. A tiny kitten doesn't know the true extent of her powers when she's brought face to face with a small black pig in this strange clip from Russia which pushes all the right "cute" buttons. Typically sows lie on their sides as they feed their piglets, so there may be a perfectly sensible reason for the pig's sudden reaction. But the possibility that the kitten, still unsteady on her paws, might indeed possess disabling superpowers should not be completely discounted!

http://y2u.be/Uu7Op0IAZRg

CALM DOWN YOUR CAT

Simple, effective and totally pain-free technique to get them under control

---

Trying to train a cat can be a thankless task. They are unpredictable balls of energy. You can never be certain what they are going to do next, which is all part of their charm. Nonetheless, it's good to have a calming trick or two ready — especially if an animal is as hyper as the kitten at the start of this video! The clothes peg replicates the way mothers carry their kittens by the scruff of the neck. The kitten's response is instant and instinctive — to chill out and let his "mother" take control.

http://y2u.be/Mu7aPLc0Lq4

FAT CAT

Dry food diet beckons for this oversized tabby

Annie was rescued when she was a kitten. Safe in a new home, she quickly became attached to a terracotta pot and loved to play and hide inside it. Unfortunately, Annie got so comfortable in her new surroundings that she started to put on some weight. Gradually it became harder and harder for her to hop in and out of her beloved pot. But Annie is nothing if not determined, and refuses to give up on her favourite hideaway. The cost of her increasingly desperate attempts to manoeuvre her now-supersized behind into position? Nothing but a little bit of dignity.

http://y2u.be/EHwu-H_KtfU

SPRINKLES GETS A SHOCK

Warning: Popping corn may cause flashbacks

A surprising addition to the list of household appliances that can send cats into a spin — the popcorn maker. At first Sprinkles is entranced; perhaps he finds the regular revolutions therapeutic. The ever-so-slightly raised paw hints that he might think this is an exciting new toy to play with. Then the action takes a sudden, dark and noisy turn. As one kernel pops loudly, then another, and another, it's all too much for Sprinkles to take. His reaction led one YouTube viewer to comment that it looked like "the cat was having flashbacks from Vietnam."

http://y2u.be/PnJo7d-xBjY

PLEASE WAKE UP!

Who needs an alarm when you've got a cat?

Some cats are early risers and their insistent cries for attention often mean their owners are forced to get up early too. Bubbles adopts a softly, softly approach to his morning wake-up calls. It's considerate, but very sweetly ineffective – this is one heavy sleeper. Bubbles' adorable bedside manner led to his inclusion alongside a number of other clips in a YouTube advertisement for a new laptop computer. The ad has received just over a million views to date. The story of Bubbles patiently waiting for his slumbering hero to wake? Almost 11 million.

http://y2u.be/n_-HKkEXkGY

BROTHERLY LOVE

Frolics in the feline equivalent of a soft play centre

In 2013, scientists researching the genome sequence of tigers made a startling announcement. As part of their efforts to save the endangered species, they discovered that the predatory big cat shares a whopping 95.6% of its DNA with the domestic cat. The strength of the ties in the cat family are on show in this behind-the-scenes footage taken at an animal reserve, where a domestic cat is very much at home alongside a tiger cub. Completely oblivious to the camera flashes and the voices of the spectators around them, these two just want to have fun.

http://y2u.be/x7Bo0wleT7o

GOLIATH'S STORY

Giant cat saved from himself

With often no way of knowing where their next meal is coming from, stray cats need to know how to look after themselves. This canny cat must have thought he'd hit the jackpot when he discovered a garage full of pet food that he could access as he pleased. It's not clear exactly how long he had been taking advantage of the stash, but looking at him, it must have been a while! His secret was revealed only when the garage owner found him wedged in the (dog-sized) entrance flap. She took him to a shelter where staff — understandably — named him Goliath.

http://y2u.be/fN7eXTz35dI

THE LICK OF LOVE

"I think she loves me back"

All who despair at their cat's indifferent behavior, look away now.
This cat is besotted and doesn't care who knows it. And it isn't
just a one-off outpouring of affection. According to Halim Amori,
who uploaded the video, this happens every single evening. Halim
explains that he studies at night and it is while he's making coffee
in the kitchen that Mia drops her delightful feline love bomb.
He says, "I love her so much and I think she loves me back…"
Watch this from start to finish, and it's very hard to disagree.

http://y2u.be/kPb6HLrNN2A

GOTCHA!

Caught in the act

It's a case of "while the owner's away" for this mischievous
Russian cat. Taking advantage of the opportunity to explore,
he wastes no time in getting started. Something's clearly
got his attention in the drawer and he has just got his paws
on the mystery orange object when – uh oh   he is well and
truly busted! His instant reaction is fantastic. It's almost
possible to see the list of plausible excuses forming in his furry
head before he slinks off. However, his show of remorse is so
charming it's unlikely he'll be in trouble for long.

http://y2u.be/gVsl3Jz4d8c

CAMERA SHY

This elegant cat is not alone

There are some things we'd all rather do in peace, far away from prying eyes. Chanel is perfectly happy on the windowsill, licking her toy and oblivious to the fact that she's being watched, until she's interrupted right in the middle of her cleaning routine. Her bashful reaction once she clocks the spectator is very, very cute. As anyone who has ever tried to create a cat video that just *might* go viral can attest, it's near-impossible to get cats to cooperate with a camera. Sometimes the only option is to try and catch them unawares.

http://y2u.be/PJMuGfm82Oc

EMERGENCY CUTE KITTEN

Stressed? Tired? Overworked? Look at cats on the internet!

Cats have huge cultural significance in Japan, where they are viewed as paradoxical creatures, both sacred and cursed, as well as symbols of good fortune. The country's obsession is reflected in the popularity of "cat cafés" – where people who don't own a cat themselves can go to relax and play with the animals. For anyone who can't get to a cat café, then there's YouTube. If you've had a bad day at work and need to unwind, there are countless Japanese videos dedicated to not much more than cats – often kittens – being ridiculously cute. Here's a prime example.

http://y2u.be/ngsmFRdbq_k

WIGGLE

Born to dance to this tune

Just before cats launch into a forward leap, they move their hind legs in a very distinctive way. It's a ritual behaviour that can be seen throughout the family – from lionesses waiting to pounce on unsuspecting prey in the wild, to domestic cats about to fly through the air in pursuit of a toy. There's a real evolutionary explanation behind the funny move. Cats are not just wiggling their bottoms for the sake of it. That said, when Jason Derulo released the horribly catchy "Wiggle" featuring Snoop Dogg in May 2014, it didn't take long for the cat video spoofs to surface.

http://y2u.be/O6ROCaLvMnQ

BAD CAT

Nothing is safe on this coffee table

When Jennifer Morales titled this video *Gato Malo*, meaning simply "bad cat", she wasn't being overdramatic. If this 35-second snapshot is anything to go by, life with this coffee table tyrant must be tough. He has no respect for remote controls and as he paws a glass towards the table's edge it looks like it's about to suffer the same fate. Morales begs him to stop, rising panic in her voice. He pauses. He turns to look at her. And then, completely and utterly unmoved by her pleas, proceeds to knock it off anyway. An unapologetically bad cat.

http://y2u.be/LNWjZcbv2uI

SO TIRED

Kitten can't keep his eyes open

Ironically enough, given the link between electronic devices and sleep difficulties, many people look to the internet if they have difficulty in dropping off. From lullabies to soothe a crying baby and videos with the sound of falling rain on a loop, to meditation music and tropical rainforest noises, YouTube is full of offerings designed to kickstart the sleep cycle. If all else fails and you still can't slip into a slumber, maybe watching an incredibly cute kitten trying to get some sleep while his siblings play excitedly around him will do the trick?

http://y2u.be/2CNd6OGdMO8

KITTEN JAM

"Fire up that loud, another round of shots"

"Turn Down for What" was the seventh biggest-selling single of 2014 in the United States. DJ Snake and Lil' Jon's popular party anthem found a pair of extremely unlikely fans in the shape of Tulip and Daisy, two rescue kittens waiting to be fostered in Arlington, Virginia. The beat-happy duo certainly know how to get down to this tune in praise of a full-on hedonistic lifestyle. It didn't take long for the video of their tiny heads bobbing in perfect time to the song's 100 bpm rhythm to go well and truly viral.

http://y2u.be/_TxV4dkRi8M

A CHIPMUNK'S REVENGE

Confused cat attacked by his dinner

Most cat owners will be familiar with the gruesome sight of dead animals left on the doorstep – or worse still, brought into the house – as (not especially welcome) gifts. Even if a cat enjoys delicious food every day, their natural predatory instincts mean they will still enjoy hunting for prey. This cat may be called Tiger, but his survival instincts leave a little to be desired. After the thrill of the chase, he starts to toy with his "dinner" – but the tiny chipmunk has other ideas. It's not just cats who can bust out ninja moves to get themselves out of sticky situations.

http://y2u.be/EOvPO8mW1Mw

Leabharlanna Poiblí Chathair Bhaile Átha Cliath
Dublin City Public Libraries